GEORGE HERBERT

POEMS

Chosen
and Introduced
by

DAVID GASCOYNE

GREVILLE PRESS PAMPHLETS

First published in this edition 2004
by the Greville Press
  6 Mellors Court
  The Butts
  Warwick
  CV34 4ST

ISBN 0 906887 87 9

FOREWORD

Before I met David, I used to give poetry readings for Hospital Radio. George Herbert was always high on the list. Like Shakespeare, the more you read his work, the more you understand it. And Herbert's poems need to be read aloud.

Soon after I had met and fallen in love with David, he mentioned that George Herbert was his favourite poet. He often talked about us giving a reading of Herbert's work together. Sadly that didn't happen.

So I am deeply grateful to Dr Roger Scott for finding and bringing to light the essay and selection David planned half a century ago in two notebooks.

I would like to conclude with a quotation from Herbert's *The Flower*:

> *Who would have thought my shrivel'd heart*
> *Could have recover'd greenness? [...]*
>
> *And now in age I bud again,*
> *After so many deaths I live and write;*
> *I once more smell the dew and rain,*
> *And relish versing: [...]*

Judy Gascoyne
25 September 2003

GEORGE HERBERT

Preface and Introduction

By David Gascoyne

Edited by Roger Scott

David Gascoyne's abiding concern at the end of the 1930s was to articulate a coherent 'vision of man's present spiritual crisis and of the future'. [1] The publication in 1943 of *Poems 1937-42* established his individual mature voice and his emergence as a major religious poet: religious preoccupations lie at the heart of the new collection with its Christian reference, and not solely in the 'Miserere' sequence which forms the first section. The visionary rubs shoulders with a lyrical intensity. So many of these poems, despite the evident anguish and despair, are lit by a radiant light which underscores the possibility for man to transcend the darkness of this world.

Gascoyne spent a year in postwar France from 1947-48. When the third impression of *Poems 1937-42* came out in 1948 he was preparing a collection which would be published in 1950 as *A Vagrant and other poems*. He listed both new and projected poems in each of two notebooks [Add.56057, Add.56058] now in the British Library Manuscript Department, [2] in which he also planned a selection of George Herbert's verse. Gascoyne drafted an introductory essay in two parts, never revised, which I have termed 'Preface' and 'Introduction' in my transcription which is lightly edited. He included a list of poems with each piece.

Some five years later, he made his lifelong admiration for Herbert very clear in a broadcast, 'Personal Anthology: chosen and introduced by David Gascoyne', transmitted by the BBC Third Programme on Monday 4th May 1953. He selected the poem 'Church-rents and schisms' to represent Herbert.[3]

Roger Scott
Northumbria University

PREFACE
'Specifically Christian poetry'

George Herbert is one of the most valuable representatives of specifically Christian poetry in English Literature. Poets who are specifically and continually Christian form a comparatively small proportion of those whose work makes up the essential history of English poetry. At the same time, English poetry as a whole is, from its Anglo-Saxon antecedents onwards, permeated throughout with Christian feeling. There is hardly a single poet of any importance at all in whose work one may not find at least one poem of which the theme is seriously religious (representing in a great many cases, a contribution valuable for its authenticity and independence to the special inner Anglican tradition of religious thought - liberal, anti-authoritarian, anti-bourgeois, philistine, patriarchal, pastoral and idyllic), a tradition firmly rooted in the English love of the Bible as inspiring poetry, and intimate personal familiarity with the words of the Gospels.

But what I mean by the term, specifically Christian poetry, is a quite small and distinct category, of which the chief representatives, besides Herbert, are Langland, [Robert] Southey, Nicholas Grimald, Stephen Hawes, [William] Drummond, Vaughan, Traherne, Smart, Hopkins and Patmore – Christina Rossetti should also be included here, although I doubt whether her poetry as a whole can be said to give a balanced integral vision of the Christian life.

4

Religious poetry, in the sense in which I understand the term, is above all the poetry of praise and represents the triumph of faith and joy over the Romantic temptation yielding to which has elegy as its first fruit. It can only be written by the stout-hearted and those whose happy childhood has left them with something of the basic relation of affectionate trust and confidence with the rest of humanity, which also makes it possible to believe that man is at home in the Universe. Romantic poetry always shows man as an alien heroically struggling against a hostile or coldly indifferent Universe, though in certain aspects of Romanticism (precisely those which make it possible to speak of specifically Christian Romanticism – Novalis, Calvert and Samuel Palmer are typical examples of this) we find an anthropomorphic humanizing of landscape.[4]

George Herbert may be said to show in his poetry the predominant influence of the words of Christ in his aspect of poet-teacher. The Gospels give us accounts in several passages of Christ's recorded voice, in which words are given with only slight variations by all four, but more often in two or three of the Evangelists, of which some of the most outstanding characteristics are those also of the highest forms of art, and of poetry in particular.

The Agony [5]	*Content*	*Dialogue*	*Complaining*
Redemption	*Humility*	*Time*	*The Pulley?*
Easter	*Frailty*	*Peace*	*The Cross*
Faith	*Man*	*Giddiness*	*The Glance*
Love I & II	*Affliction*	*The Storm*	*The Son??*
The Temper I	*The Quip*	*The Family*	

[Notebook Add.56057]

5

INTRODUCTION TO THE SELECTED
POEMS OF GEORGE HERBERT

It might be as well at the beginning of a note on the poetry of George Herbert, to make clear from the outset that Herbert is not a poet whom one can read purely for aesthetic satisfaction: he cannot be approached solely by means of Dr [I.A.] Richards's popular method of 'suspended disbelief', that kind of Husserlian bracketing which can convert no matter what poem to the accessibility of a phenomenon.

His is a meretricious appreciation that would seek to enjoy Herbert merely for his formal felicities and his 'delightful quaintness'. He should be read with a mind prepared to surrender wholeheartedly to the human appeal of his lines, to respond sincerely, that is to say with an unequivocal acceptance or rejection, to the Christian pleading that is so eloquent in most of his best poems, or honestly disregarded as a provincial curiosity. To read Herbert with a cynical 'however intelligent detachment, as though it were a purer poetry' (as indeed it is) is to fail to appreciate all that is most essential in it.

In making this present selection from the poems of George Herbert, I have grouped together near the beginning a number which all refer to the poetic act of creation, the poet's task, and which enable us to form a clear idea of Herbert's conception of poetry. In *The Quiddity*, for example, he reveals that the poem is for him a medium of communication with the transcendent. In the act of making poetry, he feels, 'I am with thee, and Most take all'. The making of poetry is a task constantly to be realized anew; almost, we may say, it is a duty made incumbent by the possession of a special gift of language. The fulfilment of this task constitutes for the poet his chief happiness, but it is not always easy to accomplish, and when there come periods of unproductive silence, he suffers from a continual sense of sterility and uselessness. That this is true of many poets and is not a characteristic peculiarity of Herbert's, is shown, it is interesting to note, by comparing his poem *Dullness* with Coleridge's poem *Work in Idleness* and the well-known sonnet of Gerard Manley Hopkins, *Thou art indeed just, Lord, if I contend / With thee.*

In *Providence*, we see that Herbert conceives poetry as the means by which the individual gifted with the power of articulation is able to perform the ministry of praise which all creatures constantly observe unconsciously in the very *fulfilment* of their being: all that has being praises the Creator simply by flourishing and rejoicing in all its own plenitude, as the birds that sing and the plants that put forth buds; but in poetry, the praise is doubly rendered.

That Herbert does not conceive poetry to be the result of simply a privately fulfilled function, an act of private communication with the transcendent, is shown by the very first verse of the first poem in *The Church-porch*:

7

Thou, whose sweet youth and early hopes enhance
Thy rate and price, and mark thee for a treasure;
Harken unto a Verser, who may chance
Rhyme thee to good, and make a bait of pleasure.
A verse may find him, who a sermon flies,
And turn delight into a sacrifice.

Thus, while Herbert had made no attempt to publish any of his religious poems, it cannot be argued that he wrote poetry only for private satisfaction, for himself and God alone, or what is equivalent, 'for art's sake': he undoubtedly was aware that poetry under certain conditions may become an evangelical communication. His awareness of this possibility, however, never led him to preach sermons in verse; none of his poems could justly be described as homilies. On the other hand, it may be said that there is a considerable element of calculation in several of Herbert's best poems, the 'artfulness' with which he contrives to touch the reader's feelings, to move us to an authentic, intimately felt response. This may be what most determined his technique, and led him to develop it to such an exquisite degree of precision and refinement.

The superb poem by which Herbert is invariably represented in every anthology of English poetry, *The Collar*, is a virtuoso piece demonstrating the dramatist's principal technical concern, the art of preparation. For words to be capable of being deeply moving in their effect, it is not enough that they should be sincere and fervently impassioned; the listener must be aware of their intention. In order for the writer's calculation to be able to achieve its object, it is necessary for

him to exercise his faculty of imaginative self-identification
with his hearers.

The poem is a votive tribute or a garland of flowers – the
images like flowers are woven and plaited by versification into
a pleasing, symmetrical form. God, to whose glory these
offerings are composed, is the dear Lord, the great friend, the
invisible King served affectionately and not in fear or merely
because [of] the intimidating prestige of an imperialist type of
Royalty [...]. [6]

George Herbert selection:

CONTENTS

The Church-porch (first 3 stanzas)

[Notebook: Add.56058]

ENDNOTES

1 *Collected Journals 1936-1942* (Skoob Books, 1991), p.256.
2 *Poem Projects*: 'A Vagrant'; 'Postscript After Seven Years'; 'Memorial'; 'With the Real Nails'; 'Marsyas'; 'Post War Nocturne' [Add.56057]. *New Poems 1948*: 'Rondel on Reaching the Fourth Decade'; 'To a Detested Voice'; 'Peacetime Night'; 'The Sybarite' [Add.56058].
Projected Poems: 'The Harrowing of Hell: A Cantata'; 'Spring Journey'; 'Postscript to an Elegy'. [Add.56058]. Some of the titles were changed for publication while others, tantalisingly, remained unwritten.
3 He commented in the recording: 'Anyone who has a special affection for George Herbert will be likely also to be fond of Henry Vaughan, "the Silurist". I find I cannot include in my choice a poem by one of them, without one by the other. Vaughan learnt from Herbert's *The Church-porch* probably as much as any poet ever learnt from and consciously owed to another, and his poems are full of references to themes and images of Herbert's yet it is always a pleasure to savour the different personal quality that makes Vaughan so distinctly an individual. Both poets gave unforgettable expression to the Christian spirit we owe to the English Church and to which the Church owes its essential unity in distractingly divided and disintegrating times' (page 5 of the BBC recording script). In a letter dated 18.10.35, sent to the French Surrealist poet, essayist and publisher, Georges Hugnet, Gascoyne quoted in French four 'truly magnificent lines' [last four] from Herbert's *Prayer 1* [I am indebted to Dr Alan Munton for

this information]: 'Ciel en ordinaire, l'homme bien habilé,/
La voie lactée, l'oiseau de Paradis,/Des cloches entendues
au-delà des étoiles, le sang d'âme,/Le pays d'épicer,
quelquechose qu'on comprend'.

4 This phrase, 'an anthropomorphic humanizing of
landscape', provides a key to understanding what Gascoyne
was attempting in the four original poems interpolated in
his *Hölderlin's Madness* (Dent, 1938).

5 In the titles and the selected poems I have followed the
spelling used in Ann Pasternak Slater's edition of George
Herbert, *The Complete English Works* (Everyman's Library
204, 1995). The question marks indicate Gascoyne's
indecision about the inclusion of certain titles.

6 The MS ends here.

The Quiddity

My God, a verse is not a crown,
No point of honour, or gay suit,
No hawk, or banquet, or renown,
Nor a good sword, nor yet a lute:

It cannot vault, or dance, or play;
It never was in *France* or *Spain*;
Nor can it entertain the day
With a great stable or domain:

It is no office, art, or news,
Nor the Exchange, or busy Hall;
But it is that which while I use
I am with thee, and *Most take all*.

Dullness

Why do I languish thus, drooping and dull,
   As if I were all earth?
O give me quickness, that I may with mirth
    Praise thee brim-full!

The wanton lover in a curious strain
    Can praise his fairest fair;
And with quaint metaphors her curled hair
    Curl o're again.

Thou art my loveliness, my life, my light,
    Beauty alone to me:
Thy bloody death and undeserv'd, makes thee
    Pure red and white.

When all perfections as but one appear,
    That those thy form doth show,
The very dust, where thou dost tread and go,
    Makes beauties here.

Where are my lines then? my approaches? views?
    Where are my window songs?
Lovers are still pretending, and ev'n wrongs
    Sharpen their Muse:

But I am lost in flesh, whose sugred lies
        Still mock me, and grow bold:
Sure thou didst put a mind there, if I could
        Find where it lies.

Lord, clear thy gift, that with a constant wit
        I may but look towards thee:
Look only; for to *love* thee, who can be,
        What angel fit?

Providence

O sacred Providence, who from end to end
Strongly and sweetly movest! shall I write,
And not of thee, through whom my fingers bend
To hold my quill? shall they not do thee right?

Of all the creatures both in sea and land
Only to Man thou hast made known thy ways,
And put the pen alone into his hand,
And made him Secretary of thy praise.

Beasts fain would sing; birds ditty to their notes;
Trees would be tuning on their native lute
To thy renown: but all their hands and throats
Are brought to Man, while they are lame and mute.

Man is the world's high Priest: he doth present
The sacrifice for all; while they below
Unto the service mutter an assent,
Such as springs use that fall, and winds that blow.

He that to praise and laud thee doth refrain,
Doth not refrain unto himself alone,
But robs a thousand who would praise thee fain,
And doth commit a world of sin in one.

The beasts say, Eat me: but, if beasts must teach,
The tongue is yours to eat, but mine to praise.
The trees say, Pull me: but the hand you stretch,
Is mine to write, as it is yours to raise.

Wherefore, most sacred Spirit, I here present
For me and all my fellows praise to thee:
And just it is that I should pay the rent,
Because the benefit accrues to me.

We all acknowledge both thy power and love
To be exact, transcendent, and divine;
Who dost so strongly and so sweetly move,
While all things have their will, yet none but thine.

For either thy *command*, or thy *permission*
Lay hands on all: they are thy *right* and *left*.
The first puts on with speed and expedition;
The other curbs sin's stealing pace and theft.

Nothing escapes them both; all must appear,
And be dispos'd, and dress'd, and tun'd by thee,
Who sweetly temper'st all. If we could hear
Thy skill and art, what music would it be!

Thou art in small things great, nor small in any:
Thy even praise can neither rise, nor fall.
Thou art in all things one, in each thing many:
For thou art infinite in one and all.

16

Tempests are calm to thee; they know thy hand,
And hold it fast, as children do their father's,
Which cry and follow. Thou hast made poor sand
Check the proud sea, ev'n when it swells and gathers.

Thy cupboard serves the world: the meat is set,
Where all may reach: no beast but knows his feed.
Birds teach us hawking; fishes have their net:
The great prey on the less, they on some weed.

Nothing engendred doth prevent his meat:
Flies have their table spread, ere they appear.
Some creatures have in winter what to eat;
Others do sleep, and envy not their cheer.

How finely dost thou times and seasons spin,
And make a twist checker'd with night and day!
Which as it lengthens winds, and winds us in,
As bowls go on, but turning all the way.

Each creature hath a wisdom for his good.
The pigeons feed their tender off-spring, crying,
When they are callow; but withdraw their food
When they are fledge, that need may teach them flying.

Bees work for man; and yet they never bruise
Their master's flower, but leave it, having done,
As fair as ever, and as fit to use;
So both the flower doth stay, and honey run.

Sheep eat the grass, and dung the ground for more:
Trees after bearing drop their leaves for soil:
Springs vent their streams, and by expense get store:
Clouds cool by heat, and baths by cooling boil.

Who hath the virtue to express the rare
And curious virtues both of herbs and stones?
Is there an herb for that? O that thy care
Would show a root, that gives expressions!

And if an herb hath power, what have the stars?
A rose, beside his beauty, is a cure.
Doubtless our plagues and plenty, peace and wars
Are there much surer than our art is sure.

Thou hast hid metals: men may take them thence;
But at his peril: when he digs the place,
He makes a grave; as if the thing had sense,
And threatned man, that he should fill the space.

Ev'n poisons praise thee. Should a thing be lost?
Should creatures want, for want of heed, their due?
Since where are poisons, antidotes are most:
The help stands close, and keeps the fear in view.

The sea, which seems to stop the traveller,
Is by a ship the speedier passage made.
The winds, who think they rule the mariner,
Are rul'd by him, and taught to serve his trade.

And as thy house is full, so I adore
Thy curious art in marshalling thy goods.
The hills with health abound; the vales with store;
The South with marble; North with furs and woods.

Hard things are glorious; easy things good cheap.
The common all men have; that which is rare,
Men therefore seek to have, and care to keep.
The healthy frosts with summer-fruits compare.

Light without wind is glass: warm without weight
Is wool and furs: cool without closeness, shade:
Speed without pains, a horse: tall without height,
A servile hawk: low without loss, a spade.

All countries have enough to serve their need:
If they seek fine things, thou dost make them run
For their offence; and then dost turn their speed
To be commerce and trade from sun to sun.

Nothing wears clothes, but Man; nothing doth need
But he to wear them. Nothing useth fire,
But Man alone, to show his heav'nly breed:
And only he hath fuel in desire.

When th' earth was dry, thou mad'st a sea of wet:
When that lay gather'd, thou didst broach the mountains:
When yet some places could no moisture get,
The winds grew gard'ners, and the clouds good fountains.

Rain, do not hurt my flowers; but gently spend
Your honey drops: press not to smell them here:
When they are ripe, their odour will ascend,
And at your lodging with their thanks appear.

How harsh are thorns to pears! and yet they make
A better hedge, and need less reparation.
How smooth are silks compared with a stake,
Or with a stone! yet make no good foundation.

Sometimes thou dost divide thy gifts to man,
Sometimes unite. The Indian nut alone
Is clothing, meat and trencher, drink and can,
Boat, cable, sail and needle, all in one.

Most herbs that grow in brooks, are hot and dry.
Cold fruits warm kernels help against the wind.
The lemon's juice and rind cure mutually.
The whey of milk doth loose, the milk doth bind.

Thy creatures leap not, but express a feast,
Where all the guests sit close, and nothing wants.
Frogs marry fish and flesh; bats, bird and beast;
Sponges, non-sense and sense; mines, th'earth and plants.

To show thou art not bound, as if thy lot
Were worse than ours, sometimes thou shiftest hands.
Most things move th' under-jaw; the Crocodile not.
Most things sleep lying; th' Elephant leans or stands.

But who hath praise enough? nay who hath any?
None can express thy works, but he that knows them:
And none can know thy works, which are so many,
And so complete, but only he that owes them.

All things that are, though they have sev'ral ways,
Yet in their being join with one advise
To honour thee: and so I give thee praise
In all my other hymns, but in this twice.

Each thing that is, although in use and name
It go for one, hath many ways in store
To honour thee; and so each hymn thy fame
Extolleth many ways, yet this one more.

The Church-porch
Perirrhanterium

Thou, whose sweet youth and early hopes enhance
Thy rate and price, and mark thee for a treasure;
Harken unto a Verser, who may chance
Rhyme thee to good, and make a bait of pleasure.
   A verse may find him, who a sermon flies,
   And turn delight into a sacrifice.

Beware of lust: it doth pollute and foul
Whom God in Baptism washt with his own blood.
It blots thy lesson written in thy soul;
The holy lines cannot be understood.
   How dare those eyes upon a Bible look,
   Much less towards God, whose lust is all their book?

Abstain wholly, or wed. Thy bounteous Lord
Allows thee choice of paths: take no by-ways;
But gladly welcome what he doth afford;
Not grudging, that thy lust hath bounds and stays.
   Continence hath his joy: weigh both; and so
   If rottenness have more, let Heaven go […]

The Collar

I struck the board, and cry'd, No more.
                    I will abroad.
What? shall I ever sigh and pine?
My lines and life are free; free as the road,
        Loose as the wind, as large as store.
                    Shall I be still in suit?
Have I no harvest but a thorn
To let me blood, and not restore
What I have lost with cordial fruit?
                    Sure there was wine
    Before my sighs did dry it: there was corn
        Before my tears did drown it.
    Is the year only lost to me?
        Have I no bays to crown it?
No flowers, no garlands gay? all blasted?
                    All wasted?
    Not so, my heart: but there is fruit,
                    And thou hast hands.

        Recover all thy sigh-blown age
On double pleasures: leave thy cold dispute
Of what is fit, and not; forsake thy cage,
                    Thy rope of sands,
Which petty thoughts have made, and made to thee
        Good cable, to enforce and draw,
                    And be thy law,
    While thou didst wink and wouldst not see.

Away; take heed:
I will abroad.
Call in thy death's head there: tie up their fears.
He that forbears
To suit and serve his need,
Deserves his load.
But as I rav'd and grew more fierce and wild
At every word,
Me thoughts I heard one calling, *Child*:
And I reply'd, *My Lord*.

Church-rents and schisms

Brave rose (alas!) where art thou? in the chair
Where thou didst lately so triumph and shine,
A worm doth sit, whose many feet and hair
Are the more foul, the more thou wert divine.
This, this hath done it, this did bite the root
And bottom of the leaves: which when the wind
Did once perceive, it blew them under foot,
Where rude unhallow'd steps do crush and grind
   Their beauteous glories. Only shreds of thee,
   And those all bitten, in thy chair I see.

Why doth my Mother blush? is she the rose,
And shows it so? Indeed Christ's precious blood
Gave you a colour once; which when your foes
Thought to let out, the bleeding did you good,
And made you look much fresher than before.
But when debates and fretting jealousies
Did worm and work within you more and more,
Your colour faded, and calamities
   Turned your ruddy into pale and bleak:
   Your health and beauty both began to break.

Then did your sev'ral parts unloose and start:
Which when your neighbours saw, like a north-wind,
They rushed in, and cast them in the dirt
Where Pagans tread. O Mother dear and kind,
Where shall I get me eyes enough to weep,
As many eyes as stars? since it is night,

And much of Asia and Europe fast asleep,
And ev'n all Africk; would at least I might
  With these two poor ones lick up all the dew,
  Which falls by night, and pour it out for you!

Prayer 1

Prayer the Church's banquet, Angels' age,
    God's breath in man returning to his birth,
    The soul in paraphrase, heart in pilgrimage,
The Christian plummet sounding heav'n and earth;
Engine against th' Almighty, sinners' tower,
    Reversed thunder, Christ-side-piercing spear,
    The six-days-world transposing in an hour,
A kind of tune, which all things hear and fear;
Softness, and peace, and joy, and love, and bliss,
    Exalted Manna, gladness of the best,
    Heaven in ordinary, man well drest,
The milky way, the bird of Paradise,
    Church-bells beyond the stars heard, the soul's blood,
    The land of spices; something understood.